THE PARTHENON

The Parthenon

by George Hobson

Foreword by Richard B. Hays

RESOURCE *Publications* · Eugene, Oregon

THE PARTHENON

Resource Publications
An Imprint of Wipf and Stock Publishers
199 W. 8th Ave., Suite 3
Eugene, OR 97401

www.wipfandstock.com

PAPERBACK ISBN: 978-1-5326-9001-3
HARDCOVER ISBN: 978-1-5326-9002-0
EBOOK ISBN: 978-1-5326-9003-7

Manufactured in the U.S.A.   AUGUST 16, 2019

Contents

Foreword

THE PUBLICATION OF *THE Parthenon* will enable a new audience of readers to discover and savor the work of one of the remarkable Christian poets of our time. George Hobson's previously published poetry collections (*Rumours of Hope*; *Forgotten Genocides of the 20th Century*; *Faces of Memory*; and *Love Poems for my Wife, Victoria*) have reached an audience of discerning readers in the UK and in Europe, but they have not yet been widely disseminated in North America. This Wipf and Stock edition offers a fresh gathering of poems that revel in the joy of the created world, probe the pain of the human condition, and proclaim the hope of God's ultimate healing of all things.

Readers will find here a bold and distinctive poetic voice—or, rather, an ensemble of voices that express Hobson's complex vision of the world. As I have lived with these poems over time, it has seemed to me that Hobson writes with at least three different voices, in three different registers, distinct but interwoven. At the risk of oversimplifying, I will name these the voices of the *painter*, the *prophet*, and the *preacher*.

George Hobson is not literally a painter, though he is a gifted artistic photographer. But he sees the variegated created world with a painter's eye, discerning patterned epiphanies of God's joyful, prodigal grace in creation. The *painter*'s voice in these poems is the lineal heir of the psalmist who declared that "the heavens are telling the glory of God; and the firmament declares his handiwork" (Ps 19:1), as well as the heir of Gerard Manley Hopkins,

who saw that "The world is charged with the grandeur of God."
Hobson does not merely echo these mystical perceptions; he re-
peatedly discerns fresh ones:

> What is that deep sea?
> The sweep of foam down a wave's face
> Pictures unsolicited grace
> Rolling from eternity
> To cover broken time.

The painter's voice not only *describes* creation, but also, using
the poetic device of apostrophe, *speaks to* it: shells, birds, cows,
leaves, the moon, all are addressed lovingly by Hobson's poet/
painter voice.

This dialogical generosity extends also to the products of hu-
man craftsmanship and art: for example, "O Bowl," and climacti-
cally in the collection's brilliant title poem:

> Oh, ride on, great bird, rider
> Of the great waters, sea-bird poised
> On the Attic rock above the dark
> Aegean: ride on till all your stone
> has turned to dust.

In this pivotal poem, it becomes clear that all human art,
though it truly hints "at depths/Beyond the shallow pools/We
spend our lives in" (as Hobson writes in the earlier poem "Art"),
remains achingly insufficient to attain the eschatological truth that
it seeks and reflects. The painter/poet weeps at the cold, tragic
beauty of the Parthenon because its "grave harmonies in stone /
Give glimmers of another world,/whose reality you could not
know."

The second voice that speaks in these poems is that of the
prophet. In the latter part of the collection, Hobson's prophetic
voice lacerates human pretension to self-sufficiency and decries
the flattened pseudoscientific rationalism of a modernity that has
abandoned transcendence. We could also call this the voice of the
social critic, but to default to that apparently neutral terminology

would be to capitulate subtly to the very reductionism that Hobson's poetry skewers. This is more than social critique. These poems assail modernity not only because it is ugly, sterile, and alienating; these failings are but symptoms of the disease. Here, it is the voice of the anguished prophet who speaks, portraying faithlessness and desolation; this withering voice is the heir of Amos, Jeremiah, and of the T. S. Eliot who wrote "The Hollow Men" and "Choruses from 'The Rock.'" These poems portray modernity's malaise as a direct consequence of its blind flight from the God who desires to give life. The destination of that flight has proven to be a swampland covered by suffocating fog—as devastatingly portrayed in the lengthiest poem in the collection, "The Fog."

There is however, finally, another voice that sounds throughout this book, speaking in concert with the other two: the voice of the *preacher*. I do not say the voice of the theologian, though Hobson is indeed an Oxford-trained theologian. The theologian articulates the structure of doctrine, explains its grammar. These poems, however, do not explain; instead, they proclaim. Some popular Christian poets tiptoe about the margins of Christian confession, gesturing wistfully towards the traditions of a faith that they own only obliquely, or even in some cases with a certain embarrassment. For Hobson, no such indirection. With Barthian gusto, he robustly declares the truth of the faith once for all delivered to the saints, and affirms that our hope lies there and only there. In one of the collection's most moving poems, leaping dolphins in the Bay of Arcachon, recalled in memory in a time of bereavement, proclaim the resurrection of Jesus and echo the promise of Julian of Norwich (and, not insignificantly, Eliot's *Four Quartets*) that "All shall be well." For Hobson the preacher, this proclamation is not simply a matter of optimism or blind trust in a benign account of history. All shall be well precisely because Christ is risen and will come again to set all things right at last. Some readers may squirm at the proclamatory tone of Hobson's poet/preacher voice; others will rejoice in it. Either way, there is no mistaking that his poetic vision depends upon reclaiming the truth of the Christian gospel. And, as he would have us recognize, the truth of the Christian gospel is the ground of all joy and love.

I have known George Hobson for almost fifty years. He has been for me a teacher, an inspiration, and a friend. He has devoted much of his life to ministry not only in England and France, but also in settings of great suffering in Rwanda and Armenia. His poetic *oeuvre* is emerging late in his life, but it eloquently embodies hard-won wisdom. It deserves to be set alongside the luminous work of other great Christian poets of our time such as Michael O'Siadhail and Malcolm Guite. What I have written here offers a tiny taste of the rich fare of this volume. I invite you, reader, to join George at the great feast.

—RICHARD B. HAYS

George Washington Ivey Professor Emeritus of New Testament
Duke University

Part I

March Morning

Glazed ferns gleam through tenebrous fir,
Stirring memories that rise,
Like trout to glinting lures,
From root-wheels and sodden logs
Mired on the bottom of years.
Slabs of sun and shadow
Stripe a grassy roadbank
Opposite a stand of pine trees
In the hills west of the Roannais
Above the bright-shining sword
Of the River Loire.
Mid-March,
Morning,
Balsam air.
Here, there,
Birds flit,
Twitter,
Sit like notes on the staffs
Of the scores of the bare branches.
All is on the verge.
On the ridge-tops, blue surges,
Scattering bibulous cloud
Hung over from night.
Blue strides down the green valley,
Embracing the willows,

Lovely in light gowns,

Shaking their tresses,

Their lemon tresses,

Laughing in welcome.

Across the hills, meanwhile,

Like salt grains on baize cloth,

Sheep graze solemnly,

And the Charolais cattle,

Sculpted in chalk,

Stand motionless,

Outside of time.

The Bowl

Under light, O bowl, paint for me,
By dahlias and peaches interposed,
The coral edges of a tropical sea.
Reflect your maker's Maker's merriment
At costumes lent by fruits and blooms
To your curvaceous finery.

Your colors whoop like schoolgirls out of class;
Like twinned lips of lovers pulled close
By beauty's sweet force,
They quiver.

I nudge the glass,
The water stirs.
The sea on beaches at the world's end sloshes,
The lovers sway among the blossoms.
Ocean sighs.

Late sun dyes the bowl vermilion.
I jar the glass again.
Creatures spring to life, myriad.
"Father, the circus is in town—
Can we go?"
We skip all the way.

Why, this is creation!
The world's being born!
Elephants stomp through purple dahlias,
Tigers pad on beds of peaches,
Jesters quilt the glass with motley—
Shalom!

Your rim, O bowl, marks out the planet's edge;
Your oceans breed whales;
Your womb is great with clouds and plants and beasts;
In your depths nebulae gleam.

O bowl, sun-bearer, in you
Light figures the invisible.
Your harmonics paint
Heavenly frescoes;
In your radiance
Alpha echoes Omega.

Shalom

Art

Art is given to hint at depths
Beyond the shallow pools
We spend our lives in,
Dull fools,
Mincing like waders when we might sprint
And plunge into the sea!

What is that deep sea?
The sweep of foam down a wave's face
Pictures unsolicited grace
Rolling from eternity
To cover broken time.

The puffed cloud's rhyme,
With chestnut trees
That caparison summer hills
And garrison the ripening fields,
Points to sublime structures of creation.

All speaks of relation,
Transformation,
Of inherent links
Binding galaxies to the pinks
That flower on the wall outside my house.

God's grand art above
Crafts these paradigms:
Playful signs of Love
That our invention mimes.

Mountain Stream

Oh, ecstasy of the enfolding cold stream
Clasping my limbs between the hills,
Issue of the run of snowmelt
Off high peaks, rippling in rills
Down the mountains to make a silver seam!

Hour by hour the broiling sun grills
My back as I toil up rocky trails,
Through fern and fireweed, over windfall,
Under placid pines with green tales
Of light and shade and silence on the old hills.

Where the purling stream awaits me sails
An eagle, circling slowly: sign
In heaven, like Christ's bright star,
That Living Waters run here, mine
For the taking: that here the Lord unveils

His luminous glory. Waters, shine!
Quicksilver, flash! Make mountains sing!
Oh, listen! Currents rush, hissing;
Stones clunk on the bottom, thumping;
Air clamors; keen wind zithers in pine.

Waked out of heat by the sonorous ring
Of rocks and the quick-running stream,
I ease my limbs down into cold's
Bracing clasp, cold's blue dream
Of liquid motion, and, borne, go slipping

Over drowned rocks, by sunken trees,
Through a green watery medium,
Below bright bubbles chattering at the surface.
I fin, buried, and all blight
In me is drowned and swept away downstream.

Oh, I ache, recalling that ecstatic flight
Through mountain waters long ago!
There was all my youth contained
And summed; and there, in that pure flow,
Love washed me clean and folded me in Light.

Life's truth defies the river's current; so
I, going after treasures stored
In time's alluvium, bring up gems
Not lost, as feared, but just ignored,
Being, far from past, the Future's signs below.

A Moment by the Sea

One by one the gray-winged oblongs with lemon beaks
Lift on updrafts off the bay where wind knocks cliffs,
Then float, feint left, right, tilt wings, glide downwind,
Make their flight over privet, clumped pines, brambles,
While their wood-and-canvas cousins on the water below
Take the same hefting wind and zigzag seaward.

Sails like triangular mosaics stud the cobalt,
Scattered shards and flakes of blue and gold;
On the ocean's edge, where sky and water fuse in haze,
The colored patches blur and disappear.

The jigsaw bay of marble is a puzzle piece
Inserted in the worn brown perforated coastal rock.
The water's surface under wind's lash knots and wrinkles
Like the cracked rock puckering the headlands.

Waves slap shorelines and scour rock pools;
They swallow distant outcrops and seethe on reefs;
Wind shears their wooly fleece.
Near land algae stain the sea floor green,
Gulls' shadows brush the water's skin,
Diving cormorants throw up nosegays of spray.

The garrulous wind cruising in the Norfolk pines
Murmurs to the sonorous waters the secrets of Creation.
Waves and trees converse. Sea and earth, bonded,
Hung by the Creator in the void, rejoice.

Reflections

Under the river shines a parallel world.

People on balconies in the water,

A voluble audience,

Stare up at people on balconies above them,

Actors on a stage;

Smiling yellow windows in the river

Wink at their twins smiling down at them;

Diners on the underwater terrace

Toast their fellow guests on the terrace above;

The concave bridge under water nearby

Welcomes its lover hanging in air—

Water admiring stone,

Mind remembering flesh;

Trees growing upside down in the river

Dream they're standing upright on the grassy bank.

O mellow images, dream on:

Decorate recollection,

Summon merriment,

Echo laughter.

As night falls,

Go on gleaming like desire in lovers' eyes.

Painted pictures,

You celebrate conviviality,

The water of life,

Without which we should shrivel.

You bind worlds:

Lives acted on the stage of years

And the memory of lives acted on the stage of years.

Do not cease to quicken our hearts

Part II

Shells

Let us give thanks for shells.

Patterned cabins of calcium
fashioned into shallow cusps
or turned as on a potter's wheel
into hollowed humps and whorls and spiraled cones—
O shells, you are shields,
shelters for soft-fleshed creatures,
homes of lime for modest mollusks,
functional, calcareous,
as strong as castle walls,
ornate as palaces.

You are ears that hear the sea,
sieves that sift the waves,
caverns where the wash of vast waters
sounds and echoes.
You are voices through which ocean speaks,
ventriloquists through whom breaking combers murmur.
Your lumpy ellipses are like planetary orbits,
your whorls like spiral galaxies,
your parabolas parables.
On your curved contours mountains gleam;
aurora borealis shimmers on your surfaces;
you carry cosmic dust on your rounded backs,
dark blobs floating on the effulgence of stars.

Time too dwells in your intimate forms.
You sleep in the tide pools of faraway summers,
on the rocks and beaches of forgotten shores.
Clams tell of children with toy shovels
running up and down wet sand, squealing;
whelks summon memories of lonely coves
strewn with the flotsam of creation,
and a boy walking thoughtfully
where the toppled waves rush up the sand hissing
and form patterns of foam that vanish quickly
as the spent waves withdraw;
mussels, massed on rocks like supplicants,
their twin shells lifted heavenward in prayer,
evoke the heavy middle passage,
the untidy, confused, occasionally glorious struggle,
the sea's batter, the sea's gifts,
the momentous daily rhythm of the tides;
and snails, stuck on walls or inching ever so slowly,
call up lazy August afternoons
in the company of family and friends,
when camaraderie has given savor to life
and the sea and salt and sun have drowned
the sometimes scarcely bearable burden of being.

In you, shells, as I gaze on you,
all of reality assembles
and is concentrated in forms.

You are tangible objects,

smooth, rough, prickly, pointed,

delicious under my fingers,

present now to me in time, yet timeless.

You are poems made of matter,

sonatas in lime:

I am your audience.

My own times and places are contained in your music,

as well as the eons of time and unimaginable spaces of being.

On you and in you,

in your tender beauty,

all God's handiwork is mirrored;

as I consider you with love, carefully,

as I let my senses welcome you,

joy sweeps away all nagging sorrow

and floods the valley of my heart.

Ode to the Moon

That rock, the moon, is settled in the fork of an ancient oak tree
Like a stone in a sling
Waiting to be flung into the night;
Or yet like a ball in a goalie's hands, ready
To be kicked downfield to the ring
Of pale stars hovering on the edge of light.

Unearthly, the globe becomes imagination's playground
And changes into anything
At fancy's nod: a round arena
Holding angel choirs, say, who, white-winged, sound
Notes from spheres unseen, echoing
The sun, as recordings of an opera

Carry voices of the original ensemble.
Like gauze, the praise floats white
On wood and field, bleaching the black
Air empty of primary light, a-tremble
Under the soft wind's slight
Flutter, like a loved cat splayed on its back,

Receiving gentle strokes. A silver platter polished
By the absent sun, free
Now from its branch, transformed, the moon
Gleams proudly in its ebony dresser, burnished

Like a warrior's shield: trophy—
Soon claimed back—of night's defeat of noon.

Utter night! Light other than light! On dreaming ground
Drops moon's mute word,
Breath lacking speech, a pallor
Like the unlight of an unworld drowned
Under lost leagues of unheard
Sound, shadowy tones, devoid of color.

Nightbirds call in the spectral moonshine. Bat wings whirr
In the gossamer air, tapping
Farmhouse windows washed with milk,
Where rays of moon paint bedroom floors, stir
Bodies sunk in sleep, wrapping
Them up, spellbound, in lustrous silk.

Such silk pictures grace, borne by the mediating moon
To mortals shivering
In deadly night, whom unclothed love,
Like original fire, would consume, as noon's
Bare blast would burn up all things having
Being as a gift, bestowed by God above.

Sacramental sign of Christ's won war
Over hell, the moon host
Brings to broken hearts bright

Hope of glory, emblem, like Bethlehem's star
Above the crib, of joy in utmost
Heaven, which banishes old night.

Glow on, round bloom, glad face of heavenly peace,
Whose silver smile, like a dove,
Translates to our faint hearts the gold
Of day, sun's glory, and grants release
From gloom, figuring sweet love
With metaphors that riddle cosmic cold.

Earth is Wet With Light

Water, water—

Water.

Wet.

Everywhere light-wet.

This is what it seems like

The sky is a great sea,

Bluebell blue,

Blue like the eyes of a Greek god.

Light rains down,

Pours from heaven:

Light-pour!

Downpour!

Drenched earth shines,

King Sun reigns.

Needle-leafed evergreens standing guard

On the deciduous populations

Of maple, oak, beech, and birch

Glitter like soldiers bedecked with medals.

Sheep flower in the meadows,

Duplicating the hedgerows of blackthorn.

Auvergnat cows are chips of dark chocolate on green tablecloths.

Holsteins trace black and white maps on the fields,

Showing continents here, oceans there.

They locate us in space.

"We are *here*," they say.

"But there is also a *there*,

And it may be quite different."

The cows stand rooted like trees,

Chewing their cuds.

Their mouths move like metronomes.

"We measure *chronos*," they say.

"But you in the act of admiring us now,

You considering us with your eyes and your pen,

That is *kairos*—

It reflects eternity."

Oh, wise cows!

Like rain revealing the color of sycamore bark,

Light's rain unveils the glory of flowers.

Magnolia blossoms are pink like the ears of pigs.

Clematis is lavender,

Iris purple,

Tulips magenta.

Cornelian cherry goes yellow in March,

Crab apple goes white in April.

In May gorse gilds embankments,

Buttercups gleam in the meadows like gold coins,

Dandelions radiate like baby suns.

There is a dance going on out there:
Everything is swinging in the downpour of light.
Catkins on the hazel and walnut trees dangle;
On the ground they turn into earthworms and wriggle.
Swallows waltz, magpies tango,
Doves foxtrot in the treetops.
A bee's shadow bebops on a white stucco wall,
A spider glides along its silken web.
Grass snakes slither curvaceously,
Lizards do push-ups.

The air is full of music.
Just listen to the woods:
Rat-tat-tats, tweets, chirps,
Staccato chattering,
Shrill piping,
And thrushes carrying the melody.

It is time for celebration.
Light's downpour is watering the world,
Everything is bursting.
On the green hills, horses buck and whinny;
Cud-chewing cattle provide *basso continuo*.
In the meadows, lambs scamper and hop,
They thrust at their mothers' udders and yank,
They wiggle their tails and guzzle.
In the fields, under wind,

Crops wave and ripple.
A few early vegetables in well-tended gardens
Poke their heads up and blink.
The trees on the hills and in the dales,
Standing in the hollows and along the streams,
Laugh and shake their leaves gaily;
The poplars giggle.
Light's downpour is watering the world.

Oh, summer!

Green Surf

Waves of low hills roll westward to the end of the earth.

Silently, billows of green surf tumble into yellow flat fields,

The brown froth of heat-parched oak-leaves bubbling in the green.

The wave at earth's end is a band of indigo blue;

As a dream laps the conscious mind,

The dark band laps the pale sky.

Cloud shadows charcoal the waves of hills:

Now they smudge them,

Now they seem to mold the bundled trees like clay.

High above,

As on a parallel sea,

Float the grand puffy clouds themselves,

Insubstantial yet light blocking,

Like ephemeral emotions, potentially ominous,

Capable of darkening the heart.

Under the itinerant cloud forms the shadows shift,

But without seeming to.

They stain the fields,

They knead the hills,

Yet their motion is hardly perceptible:

It is like plants growing—

You see that they *have grown*,

You do not see them growing.

And for all the high drama—

The tumble of green waves,

The churn of brown surf,

The shadow hands of white clouds sculpting hills,

Inking fields—

Not a sound is to be heard.

The wind itself looks on in silence,

A spectator,

Transfixed.

The Generations

I

Go tell all those plum-tree blooms
To fill the holes in your unmothered heart.
May they snow down heaps on your charred ground!
Speak to the breaking waves of blackthorn:
"Waves, go! Churn my fields! Pump life
In my unirrigated soul!"
The gold that flares in the prickly gorse veining the fields
Can make your poor heart rich;
The butter of forsythia is unguent
For eyes grown red with weeping.
Listen to the jazz in the walnut trees—
Those glad birds can make the cornfields swing
And the green stalks rock in stony soil!

II

You must endure the bleat of mocking goats,
Who know nothing, understand nothing,
Yet bleat.
Women who throw verbal knives deserve your kindness—
Who else will love them?
Idolatrous men in swivel chairs who smile condescendingly
Will soon feed worms—
Empty oil drums,

These too may find mercy.

Lord, have mercy on me, a sinner

And you must bear reports of slaughter,
And thank Jesus for Calvary,
And pray,
And do good.

The violent die violently,
None knows what he is doing—
Not *really*.
You must endure.

III

From generation to generation

A cat pours off a garden wall in England
A wild horse whinnies in Mongolia
In the Southern Sea a squid squirts ink
A bull moose bellows in the Rockies
From a stream in Nepal a panda rakes fish
A llama paws snow in the Andes
Rhinoceroses thunder on the Serengeti Plain

I remember horses whinnying in my childhood
On prairies covered with purple sage;

And antediluvian brontosauruses

Nibbling treetops;

And rhinoceroses thundering on the Serengeti Plain

Rhinoceroses

Thundering

IV

Out at sea whales call to each other.

Their cry is like the cry of loons on northern lakes,

The cry my heart makes remembering joy.

When my hair was still black,

I saw dolphins leaping in the Bay of Arcachon.

I was on holiday with a strong-armed friend

Who loved to sail dinghies.

Once a captain took our families fishing in his boat.

We fished some cousin of the sardine.

They loved my friend's bait,

He caught dozens;

His son caught none and brooded aft.

Ah, the generations!

Fathers, mothers, sons, daughters:

Blood's ambiguities;

Jealousies, rivalries, longings:

Love's labyrinths.

From generation to generation

Innocence like gossamer on grass in morning—
Quickly gone;
Yet—like beasts—outside of time.

V

That was when we saw the dolphins rolling
Toward the open ocean.
They broke water rhythmically for a thousand yards,
Rising and plunging.
"He has risen!" we heard them calling.
"He died and has risen."
And: "All shall be well."
Like black torpedoes they arced up,
Scattering haloes of sea drops,
Then dove and rose again,
Again and again,
Joyous.

VI

Years have passed.
My friend died suddenly last winter, aged forty-six.
Now his widow stands by the window at Arcachon,
Their son beside her.
She remembers the black dolphins
And seems to see them in the bay again

Rolling toward the open ocean.

In slow motion through her tears

They lift above the dark water,

Creatures from the deep,

Great bodies shimmering like angels,

Rising, plunging,

Wreathed in glory.

"Sad heart," she hears their cry.

"Be still, it is well."

And the bell buoy tolling:

"It is well, it is well."

And the dolphins and buoy together:

"All is well:

He has come, he will come:

All love shall live in Him

And flame again:

All things shall be well."

Part III

The Parthenon

Once, when I was a young man,
I wept to see the Parthenon
Riding its terraced plates of stone
Like a sea bird on an ocean swell,
Poised above the dark Aegean
That fated Agamemnon furrowed
In the Heroic Age, when the world
Was younger than it is today,
Younger even than it was
When Ictinus raised the Parthenon
High above Athens. Homer's world
Was wilder, more barbarous
Than the world of Pericles.
His armored heroes walked and talked
With the Olympian immortals,
And slew each other. Their code was simple.
By taking their destinies to be
Determined, they made a harsh kind
Of sense of their brief trek
Across the plain of the living. Lacking
Hope, they quaffed the wine of myth.
Their bright earth was polished by wonder
As by moonlight; it trembled, like morning,
With the dew of beauty. Men loved
The visible forms of things, surfaces,

The clear, precise light of day.

Yet in their soul, below ground,

An echo of ancient betrayal

Reverberated ceaselessly:

The memory of broken trust,

Of violence and bloodshed,

Requiring perpetual revenge

Or an unimaginable atonement.

Millennia later, on seeing Athena's

Temple, built when lordly Hellas

Had taken to itself the task

Of civilizing the imagination

And establishing the Olympians in Athens,

I wept, as though defined somewhere

Deep in my humanity,

On some hardly accessible

Level of my inner being,

By this awesome, distant splendor.

The great fluted Doric columns,

Lifting the entablature to the blue

Vacancy of the Attic sky,

Stood like trees of the human spirit,

Icons of immaculate Being,

Perfectly presenting to sight

The orchard of intelligible Forms.

Yet that is no orchard to walk in.
It is as cold there as here.
No ideal Form or Notion can
Remove our bleak mortality
Or atone for man's rank pride.
The shadow of the primal sin falls
Dark on Greece's Golden Age,
No less than on the old Heroic
Age of Homer. Here is no final
Peace, no reconciliation:
Only reality challenged by reason.
Under the glory crouch the Furies;
The spiral is still unbroken.
These marble shafts are self-contained,
Like Polycleitus's athlete,
That dream-eyed warrior-youth,
Poised, perfect, with a stony stare
As blank as the ether beyond the moon.

The Alone calling to the alone.

No, in the orchard of intelligible Forms
One does not take a picnic. I wept
At such unembraceable beauty.
We cannot grasp a rainbow. Everything
Passes. The deer bounds into the woods,
You will never hug its firm neck;

The collie that nuzzled your face
When you were a child, died long ago;
The girl with lips of coral and lashes
That made you tremble with desire,
Married and moved to another city:
Only her husband tastes those lips,
Only he knows how she is made
(And that is as it should be);
But you who took the keen arrow
Of her beauty in your heart, suffer,
Craving the Beauty she embodied
Yet powerless to embrace it,
As a stream flowing in a wood cannot
Embrace the trees shining on its surface.
Whose is the face in the window?
On the jetty, waving? Whose, there,
In the lamplight under falling snow?
On the metro, as the train leaves
The underground station? On paths
And benches in parks in old cities
You have seen Helen and Dido,
Guinevere, Cleopatra,
Francesca, Juliet, Lara:
They have not known you saw them,
Arm in arm with their lover or leading
Their children under the green foliage:
A flare of hip, breast's swell,

Nipple's rise, the curve of belly,
A leg's round trunk, hand's flutter,
The liquid gleam of eyes, lid's
Shutter, white clouds of laughter,
An arch tilt of brows, a shoulder's
Roll, the weight, coil, drop,
The toss, drift, swirl of thick hair:
And you have felt the sea boil
And seen stars fall out of the sky.

The longing for a particular person
(Or thing) points beyond the person
To a Particular who also is
Infinite, who satisfies
All true desire, setting love's
Bentness right, purging hunger,
Restoring purity. Lacking
Divine disclosure of the Personal God
Who became Man and dwelt among us,
One can't imagine such a Being;
One suffers pain inside the limits
Of the changing, elusive, not fully
Graspable singular, and yearns
For release into the universal
Under some guise or other,
Such as Polycleitus's warrior-
Athlete, planted beyond loss,

Beyond time and the battlefield

(The Alone calling to the alone);

Or Phidias's golden Athena,

The goddess captured in ivory

(The statue was destroyed long ago);

Or the noble Parthenon itself,

Standing like a metaphysical statement

Between sky and stony land,

The empyrean and solid earth,

Emptiness, where Ideas dwell,

And the transient, tangible ever-

Flowering, ever-passing world.

All we love, for an instant or

A lifetime, goes over the hill

Like the traveler, or flits among

The shades of memory's dreamscape;

And what we fail to love does not

Exist for us really, though it cries

Out, like all things in creation,

To be recognized and embraced.

The universal must be given

In the Person who is infinite

And who made human beings in his image.

All forms point to Form, but that

Is not the end: Form itself

Points to God who fashioned it,

In whom all beauty has its Source.

Oh, ride on, great bird, rider
Of the great waters, sea bird poised
On the Attic rock above the dark
Aegean: ride on till all your stone
Has turned to dust. Your gold goddess,
Despite the bell-tongued Aeschylus,
Failed to appease the Furies or efface
Old sin. Athena was not Christ.
Yet your grave harmonies in stone
Give glimmers of another world,
Whose reality you could not know.
I wept, seeing your splendor to be
Tragic.
Needless tears. *He has come.*
Now the vision of God's kingdom
Lifts before my longing eyes:
There, in that other, glorious realm,
Shown to faith more truly than to intellect,
Real persons, men and women,
Transformed and cleansed from ancient guilt,
Stand tall as life-filled columns,
In dignity and royal peace,
In a temple greater than the Parthenon,
Majestic, imperishable,
Built not by human hands or minds
But by the Spirit of the living God,

The holy, true, everlasting One,
Creator and Lover of men.

Again I weep, beside myself.
That surge of joy, as I beheld
So long ago the wondrous temple
On the Attic rock—joy dashed
So swiftly by death's fetid breath—
Takes flesh now in solid hope
Beyond my farthest dreams, at the rim
Of the shimmering sea where Homer
Sailed, the mortal world's end,
Where our most deep-down, dearest
Imaginings, all our glimmerings
Of truth, find final fulfillment
In immortal communion,
Outlasting the combustion of stars.

The Vision: Emmanuel Church, Greenwood

I

God's Spirit sowed a vision in six hearts
In the wake of the birth of a bouncing boy to Mrs. Davis,
Wife of the Reverend D. C. T. Davis, a minister
From Charlottesville, friend of the widow Garrett,
On the occasion of a service conducted by her husband
At Clover Plains in Albemarle, to which
The Davises had come by train, the recently completed
Virginia Central line across the mountains, the trip
By horse and buggy being impossible
For someone in Mrs. Davis's condition,
The return trip being equally impossible
Until Mrs. Davis had recovered.

Her husband and the widow Garrett, an Episcopalian,
Along with the physician, Dr. Rice,
Talked for many long hours over tea
About their dream to build a church in the region.
The brothers Bowen, Thomas and James,
Soon joined them with their wives,
Making six local people with a vision
And a friend they could call to be rector.
All this came together in their hearts
In the wake of the birth of Mrs. Davis's boy.

The birth of a child, the birth of a vision:
Here were the beginnings of Emmanuel Church.

II

The following April Fort Sumter was shelled.

Men were rapidly mobilized.
Drums, fifes, tears,
Lots of waving of handkerchiefs,
Loud cheering and whooping—
The romance of war!
Oh, how little they knew,
How little they knew.

Where grand oaks grew in Greenwood,
Albemarle County, Virginia,
The land had been acquired,
Bricks and mortar were being assembled.
Construction of the church began.
Everyone expected the conflict would be short.

At Bull Run, McDowall faced Beauregard.
The untrained troops fought stoutly.
Gaggles of Washington civilians came out to view the show,
Imagining a sort of rugby match with shooting.
From the nearby hills they watched the cannon smoke
And ate cakes.

Their conveyances met the wagon trains and artillery

Of the retreating Union army

On the roads leading back to the city.

A stray Confederate shell struck a wagon,

Blocking the bridge on Cub Run.

Panic seized the green recruits and the holiday-makers.

Things fell apart,

Pandemonium ensued.

Nearly five thousand men died that day.

The picnic was over.

Soon tens of thousands of young men were enlisting.

Volunteer regiments were recruited and trained.

To the east and south of Greenwood

Troops crisscrossed the land.

Armies clashed.

Jackson faced McClellan in the Shenandoah.

Mortars shuddered on the mountains.

Came Shiloh to the west;

Came Antietam.

The gashed land ran blood.

Meanwhile Emmanuel Church at Greenwood was rising,

Ringed round by spreading oaks.

Hope appeared and reappeared

Like the moon at night amidst moving clouds.

Prayer battled horror.
The six persevered.

Came Lincoln's Proclamation:
Emancipation for the slaves!
The boil was punctured—
The pus would be a long time seeping.

Came Fredericksburg,
Chancellorsville,
Vicksburg.
Burnside, Rosecrans, Bragg, Hooker, Lee, Grant, Meade battled.
The Federal and Confederate armies battled.
Brothers battled.
Hundreds of thousands of men were fighting,
Tens of thousands were dying.
Batteries of big guns pounded enemy battalions,
Shrapnel flayed attacking infantry.
Young men sank down dead,
Horses writhed,
Farms went up in flames.
Death slouched in the mud and blood.

Virginia and Tennessee were dyed red.

Then came Gettysburg.
A. P. Hill swept in from the west.

Meade held.

Lee stumbled.

The third day the Confederate mortars overshot the Union troops on

Cemetery Ridge

(The ridge was aptly named).

Pickett's climactic charge was a hecatomb.

Half a hundred thousand men fell in three June days.

"Four score and seven years ago our fathers brought forth on this continent, a new nation, conceived in Liberty, and dedicated to the proposition that all men are created equal. Now we are engaged in a great civil war, testing whether this nation, or any nation so conceived and so dedicated, can long endure. We are met on a great battlefield of that war . . . "

A Voice cries:

"You shall endure, O land, and flourish,

So long as you trust your God,

So long as you cleave to the Christ who brings salvation,

So long as you act justly and seek the common good."

On Christmas Day, 1863,

While the war was still raging

And men were slaughtering each other,

The Reverend D. C. T. Davis held the first Eucharistic service

At Emmanuel Episcopal Church in Greenwood,

Albemarle County, Virginia.

In this new church named after him,

The Lord Jesus—*God with us*—presided.

Fifteen persons took communion.

III

As the coming of the baby Jesus—

Peace-bearer from heaven—

Was immediately challenged by Herod's decree

To massacre all infants in Jerusalem under two years old,

So the vision to build a Christian place of worship in Greenwood,

Where the peace of God through Christ could be proclaimed,

Was immediately challenged by the outbreak

Of the frightful Civil War.

For four years America burned.

Everywhere was conflagration, wreckage.

The soldiers bore pain beyond telling.

Great fortitude was shown.

In April 1865, the war ended.

The South was ruined.

Grant and Lee made a fair peace at Appomattox.

The armies disbanded,

The soldiers trickled home.

Men struggled to reconcile magnanimity and bitterness.

Then Lincoln was assassinated by a fool,

And the nation staggered.

The Furies were active.
God's blessing on the damaged American experiment
Would continue to be challenged.

But the Union had survived.
The institution of slavery was abolished,
The founding vision of the nation was confirmed.
A tragedy had befallen America—
God's judgment was plain to see—
But meaning was to be found in it,
God's mercy overcame his wrath.

As it is written: *"Where sin increased, grace abounded all the more."*

IV

The church in Greenwood, symbol of divine grace,
Did not cease to worship God throughout the war.
Its roots were put down in the midst of suffering;
Its faith held.
Emmanuel has flourished ever since,
Preaching mercy, forgiveness, reconciliation.
Without this preaching, we must stray like lost sheep,
Now as then.

In our blackness, where death reigns,
The Author of Life took human form: *God with us.*
The death our sin incurs, he shouldered.

In his body on the Cross, death died.
So it is written: *"Where, O death, is your victory?*
Where, O death, is your sting?"
For Christ rose from the dead—
He lives!

And here on Greenwood Hill, where the Great Oak,
Like God the Father, spreads its limbs to shade
The church devoted to the Son; here where the grand trees
Lift their arms and clap their hands in praise,
Like the children of God at the altar gathered to worship;
Here where hope, like summer green, spreads its mantle
On the land—here God's word seeks incarnation
Once again; here divine love seeks a vessel,
Grace seeks a body by which to bless the world.

In our beginning is our vocation, our meaning

The vision to build a church for the King of Peace
Arose in Albemarle on the eve of war;
So now again today, in our age of terror,
Our age of wars and of rumors of wars,
As nation rises against nation,
Kingdom against kingdom,
The call goes out to lift high him who died
So that we might live and learn to love:
Emmanuel.

Oh, may the wind that shakes the Greenwood oaks
And makes them sing, shake us;
As we speak life to the dry bones all around,
May they come together and revive;
May the vision the faithful six received
One hundred and fifty years ago
Infuse this church anew for the century to come,
That the Christians here may glorify the Savior
And act in the power of the Spirit of God!

Prophetic Fire

There is no special time for prophecy. Budding March,
And the crocus pointing to emergent possibility,
Are not properly prophetic; nor is April's lank virility,
The flare of tulips on the green. No time to do God's will
Is privileged: all times are equally propitious.
Perhaps August's heat, when ripening plums at wind-shake
Drop, or November's blear drizzle and heartbreak
At hope's foreclosure in the year's dying fall, may be auspicious
Times to speak of judgment and unseemly death's grim yoke.
Perhaps. Or December's night, when ice-charged limbs of trees
Old and young crack in the utter cold and killing freeze
Of the winter solstice. Perhaps if the burning prophet spoke
At such a time, he might be heard. Might be. But the breath
Of God blows down life's thoroughfares in every season,
And the hearts of men have never either more or less reason
To heed the word it whispers of eternal life or death.

All seasons are prophetic and all seasons are occasions
To declare God's judgment, searching love, and rule.
The cycle of the turning year is in itself no school
Of truth; nature's repeating variations
Provide no mirror of her Lord, save only to the one who sees
Behind the flux, the Constant, behind effects, the Cause,
The Law-Giver behind the inviolable laws,
And the Current under the random vortices

Of time. Unless the prophetic word illuminates our history,

Significance is absent, even order seen lacks sense;

Unless the One who gives to the prophet the utterance

Not only speaks but acts to save our sphere, the story

Of this spinning earth is vain despite its rhymes, our tale,

Told well or poorly, but a trill in some discordant tune

Whistled by no one. But the prophet sees beyond jejune

Despair, to love's bright face: Christ, he declares, is history's Braille.

Dense

I

Let Dense fall,
It will not break,
It will plow a hole
In the earth like a meteor.

II

Dense
A cat's purr,
Fur's voice,
Puttering inside flesh,
Vibrating in muscles,
A motor idling
On a lake loved
Once
For the smell of it,
Touch,
Sight of it,
The wash,
Water's slurred speech.
Loved only in memory
Now
Abstracted from sense,
Lodged in the brain's circuitry

Now

Beside a plane droning

In summer

Summer

Remember?

Oh, buried in Old Pond,

Those who peopled it

Buried—

Summer!

Full of blue porcelain,

Cotton clouds,

Heat,

Leaf.

All in mind now,

Memory,

From solid matter lifted

And turned to matter

Light as air,

Light as the blue

Where the plane droned so high,

Now nestled in mind

Beside the cat's purr,

Motor's putter,

And—look!—

Surfacing—

A white cow

By a pea-green gate,

Being milked into a pail:
Whoosh-whoosh-whoosh-whoosh
Hmmmmmmmm
Drone
Purr
Putter—
Whoosh!
Dense.

III

And dense
Is
Glory!
Denser than
The matter of white dwarf stars.
And light,
Weightless.
Oh, light!—
Deity's substance,
Godhead's matter,
Spirit's flesh!
Dark a star's core
Beside the Light of its Maker;
Light our dense
Beside the weight of God.

IV

Oh, clothe me with light!
Transfigure my flesh!
So it shall be:
For at the sea's edge
Where the void looms,
The Son has risen.
You shall be you,
Beloved,
Forever and ever,
A man with a history
In the history of Earth;
Yet you shall be new,
George,
Forever and ever,
Death-bound but quickened
By a heavenly birth.
You are lodged in God's story,
You shall dwell in his glory.

V

Dense
Came down
Here
And walked on earth
Lightly

And plowed into it
Like a meteor
And at the end
Shouldered it
On shoulders weaker than a Jew's in Belsen,
Stronger than a titan's.

VI

The True Prometheus
Is Light:
Not the stealer of fire,
But Very Fire.
And he has planted
East of Eden
A burning bush:
And its leaves burn
But are not consumed,
And shall burn
But not be consumed,
Forever and ever

Dense

Gathered Gulls

I

The gulls gather at first light over the islands,
screeching;
with loud cries they welcome day.
As light fails, they gather again,
screeching;
they swoop and wheel above the waters,
sketching circles on the wind,
screaming.

II

What do they tell the rocks, the sea, us humans
who hear their community over the wide waters,
screaming?
Do their dawn-breaching wings sense,
beyond night,
tireless flight
on updrafts of Spirit?
As dark engulfs them
and waves roll under them,
washing and tossing,
do they grieve the wound
at the heart of the world?

Do the gulls know in their bodies that the sun is a gift
from One greater than the sun?
Do they scream through their yellow beaks
that Life must conquer,
being primary,
knowing the while nonetheless
that Life stands for the time being challenged
by the Blind Thief,
Purveyor of Darkness,
and shall be so challenged
till Time is fulfilled
and the One greater than the sun returns?

III

Is their screeching at dawn's light
laughter,
laughter of birds,
laughter of wings,
joyous and wild beyond telling,
echo from the kingdom of heaven
where the Risen Lord reigns?

Is their screaming as night drops
weeping,
a weeping—oh, such a weeping!—
as to tear up the earth,
to rip open the planet,

the whole universe grieving God's Logos,
his body ripped, broken,
hanging on the dark cross,
dying?

IV

Gulls, what do you tell us?
Your screams well up in our hearts like tears,
yet they bring good news from a far country;
they tear the soul,
yet they heal it with hope.
Great birds,
sea riders,
what mystery do you know?

V

The gulls wheel above the wide waters,
scaling the air
swooping
screaming.

At dusk and dawn
under the enormous sky
they bestride the wind,
worshipping.

The Leaf

Two-dimensional cathedral, flat
On the pavement, a thousand like it
Scattered on the wet street where a fat
Woman under an umbrella waddles slowly,
The five-lobed blotchy leaf knits
Worlds together in its green-veined fan,
Its long wings like the five-aisled plan
Of Bourges Cathedral, marking holy ground,
Where we who pass by should remove our shoes and bow.

But no one passing by removes his shoes. The shedding
Sycamore, kissed by wind, drops duplicates
Of its cathedral on the pavement, browning
The macadam with dead life. Like papyruses
That once were reeds, countless replicates—
Of which each, though alike to all, is singular,
Its harsh rasp on the rainy street oracular—
Cry out, like the petals of irises
Scattered on autumnal earth: "We give glory to God!"

But no one sees the glory. No one sights
The peaks the jagged leaf tops print upon
The banal asphalt, the pinnacled heights
Of pointy crags, the umber ridges seamed
With water courses streaming toward the stem

Of the lobed form, thick like a rat's tail,
Turbulent river cutting out a trail
Seaward through the valleys and piled up reams
Of fissured rock figured by the wondrous dead leaf.

Here are mountains. And here are radial stars
Flaring on a rainy city street and crushed
By feet, crates, trolleys, and fanatical cars
Rushing by clueless that this is cosmic soil
Colored by the yellow afterglow of lush
Stars burning in night. This dead leaf
Carries in its lobes the origins of life
Embedded in the fusion of nuclei roiling
In the incandescent cores of primordial stars.

And these leaves are birds. At the wind's behest
They swirl up from the pavement in flurries, swoop
On breezes, float, twirl, tumble with zest
Like swallows turning, tails forked, wings wide,
Then drift among their mother trees, loop
Down, settle, cluster finally in heaps.
O lobed leaf, flat cathedral, through you spirit leaps
Again, lifting your blotched body, you who died:
Thus, to those with eyes to see, you give a signal: glory!

Part IV

Modernity

The night's weight presses on my moon-wide eyes
As I lie sleepless in this house of stone
That sheltered goatherds once when stars still shone
In uncorrupted air, like fireflies,
And lilacs really bloomed before they died.
The humid dark impresses on my mind
Time's passage and its strange sterility
In this old age we call modernity
Where nothing grows but all, refined,
Mutates in vacuo, unqualified.
Such novelty, banal as habit, hangs
Like tawdry fate on human flesh and bone.
Artifice can't save. Behind our masks, alone,
We sweat. Only Christ can break death's fangs.

Things-as-they-are

No poetry will lift these littered lots
To heaven, though poets may believe that God exists;
No lively tales of palaces and kings
Will turn the deadly glass atop these walls
To jasper, emerald, or chrysolite;
Not green imagination's farthest reach
Will change these blown-out boa tires
To chariot wheels of gleaming angel hosts.

If for a moment we might see it so,
If in decay we might an instant glimpse
Decay redeemed, by water cleansed,
The cockroach-swarming cupboard of our nights
Scrubbed white,
The sky-sheened puddle in our mud-bound days
An actual chunk of blue—
Oh, if the poet's word might briefly make it so,
Yet a skip of the heart and the conjured sight would fade
Like the sense of a dead companion's presence in the room:
Things-as-they-are in our dear savaged world
Would reach out battered arms and put their claims,
Fling back at us their untransfigured names:
        "Not gems but shards,
        Not kings' abodes but yards,
        Not chariot wheels but rubber tubes

Are we."

Then we would stagger weeping down delirious streets

Aligned in rows,

And mourn as monitors stuck phials in lakes

Where bass don't breed,

While on our broken hearts came clamping down,

Like the fangs of a demented dog,

The manacles of fear.

Blight

The clock ticks in the encompassing night,
basso continuo;
The tick is like a man treading water
in the center of the ocean.

Immediacy is melted in the sea of time,
immeasurable fathoms deep;
Space is consumed in night's bleak dark,
undone in silence.

Impossible now to imagine light,
sun's overflow;
Among the dead one doesn't hear laughter
or see motion.

Reality is strewn about in rhyme-
less strophes, to make one weep;
In this blank black no shape or bark
keeps substance.

The world's sickened by encompassing blight,
death's halo;
No God goes here, no life chatters—
dissolution!

What flew and swam and jumped is caught in lime,
not even worms creep;
For our wild folly, behold Truth's
fatal sentence.

The Mind's Confrontation With Horror (Unfinished)

As the sun performs its carpentry
on the oak beams in my old house,
and the shadows lengthen along
the stone walls, announcing evening,
my mind goes to the millions even
now dying of AIDS or of famine,
being tortured in prisons or murdered
on account of their faith in Christ,
or because they were born members
of this or that ethnic group or race
or nation, or because they showed
courage in denouncing lies
or injustice or outrageous deceit,
or their presence by chance at a site
where a bomb explodes or a mine
left over from a former war
goes off in a field when a young girl
running to gather wood happens
to step on it . . . and my mind moves
back in time to the countless slaughters,
massacres, pogroms, genocides
littering history, and the vicious
trade in slaves carried on by Arabs
and Europeans and Americans

under the banners of commerce, empire,

racial superiority,

expanding civilization,

and the endless wars of conquest

of one people by another . . .

and I tremble, my brain reels,

my heart sickens and grows weak,

any sense of meaning to human life,

of purpose in the universe,

pales, the shed blood and horror

and pointless hatred and cruelty

threatens to overthrow all hope

and the very structures of sanity.

The Fog

I

Fog rolled in over the centuries, creeping down the inlets,
Investing the valleys where communities once lived,
Massing on the cliffs, covering the hills and mountaintops,
Obliterating all stars and the moon and even the golden sun,
So that we moved without reference to anything beyond ourselves
And came to deny the existence of anything beyond ourselves,
And each man and woman moved in a private reality
With a metaphysics that denied metaphysics
And an *ad hoc* ethic of convenience
Whose social end product was moral anarchy
Held in check by material possessions
And varieties of legalism.

II

With no transcendent context, relations between persons,
And between persons and other things in the world,
Grew functional and heartless.
Trust disappeared, and all certainty,
As if the rock of the world had turned to water;
Only restless movement remained, and murderous conviction.

III

We ceased to consider heavenly bodies
Other than as objects subject to description
In terms of forces and electromagnetic pulsations,
Finding in them no significance
Beyond their own discrete material composition,
Setting them in no framework
Other than that determined by their physical parameters,
As if metaphysics had become physics.
Signs and metaphors and correspondences
Were beyond our imagining,
The faculty of imagination having atrophied;
We had lost the capacity to symbolize,
All we could do was calculate and measure
In terms of the two dimensions we groped about in,
Even while, ironically, some of us talked in tacit
Metaphysical language of four dimensions or of ten,
Of spacetime, quanta, photons, and other wonders,
Phenomena we had lost all power to comprehend,
Having taken as first principle a most unreasonable notion,
Namely, that the ground of universal order is Chance,
On which patently irrational premise
We had erected our rationalism
And the accompanying rationalization of every aspect of life,
Such that we had become impervious
To the light of revelation and its explanatory power.

IV

From the ocean, over centuries, with inexorable pressure,

The fog rolled in

And shrouded the capes and promontories along the coasts.

Here and there spurs and arches of ancient cliffs,

Pines towering on rocky crags,

Oaks bunched on adamantine hills,

Resisted the enveloping mists,

Pointing skyward;

But few particularities stood fast

Against the blanketing vapor.

On the seas, boats tacked fitfully in all directions at once,

Each a law unto itself,

Like moths flitting in the night;

And on the continents billions of campfires burned in the dark,

Each stoked by a sophisticated barbarian concocting his private religion

From flotsam and fossils and rummage sale items,

With a few facts thrown in and some rumors and digital mail

That crisscrossed the dense fog ceaselessly,

Providing each migrant with a constantly changing stock of information

And the happy illusion—

Until death grinned at him

Or a child screamed somewhere in the fog

Or a wolf's eyes glinted at the edge of his campsite—

That he had a grip on reality.

V

We did not want company.

"Leave me alone," we said.

The Presence of an Other was burdensome,

So was the presence of others,

So was the presence of our own deeper self;

So we banished all these from our kingdom.

"It is better to be alone," each of us said.

Nor did we really want explanatory power

Unless the explanation was our own.

We wanted power, *tout court.*

Nothing rooted in an Origin beyond the human intellect

Was admissible.

Thus we could not integrate

The complex aspects of reality,

And chose a specious uniformity

As a counterfeit of cohesion,

And a specious autonomy

As a counterfeit of freedom.

We carried on unhappily

In a dislocated culture

In which personal trust had broken down

And from which joy had fled,

As in the vision of Ezekiel

When the Spirit of God departed from the temple:

A culture driven by its internal contradictions

And by the irrationality of its first principle

To self-destruction and wanton murder

(It was not uncommon for parents to kill children

And for children to hate parents,

And persons born with handicaps,

Or who were too old or ill to be useful,

Were systematically weeded out).

Hence even the splendor of the culture's achievements—

And they were great and many—

Failed to bring the personal fulfillment

That was supposed to accompany

Unlimited choice in a modern market economy

And unlimited individual rights in a modern egalitarian democracy:

For the ultimate Source of those achievements—

The Creator and Redeemer who had revealed himself

And welcomed men and women to live with him in love—

Had been abjured.

VI

In the case of the billions of sophisticated barbarians tending their campfires

In the pea-soup fog that reduced visibility to zero

And turned personal relationships into a matter of abstract communication,

The reigning ideology that rejected all limits to individual activity

(On the pattern of the unlimited experimentation permitted to technology),

And vaunted open horizons and endless permutation,

In fact created a world hermetically sealed off from outsiders,

Closed and turned in on itself like a snail,

From which absolute truth in the form of a Personal God was barred,

Its existence denied.

Some of the solitary campers saw the irony of this,

Yet the blindness brought on by the fog

Prevented most of them from seeing anything more

Than the fascinating glow of their own fires in the night;

And in the glow, what they saw—fog—

Did undoubtedly appear unlimited,

A fact that seemed to vindicate their ideological position

And confirm their cherished principle of absolute moral relativism,

When in reality the only thing limitless about the fog

Was the confusion it generated,

And the only thing absolute about moral relativism

Was the lie underlying it.

VII

Under the fog, life became increasingly abstract.

The sophisticated barbarians handled objects instrumentally,

At a distance,

Through the intermediary of machines.

They lost touch with wood and leaf, stalk, stone, soil, wind, water, even light,

Except as these could be packaged and sold as commodities.

Animals were turned into things and denatured.

Old trees looming in the mist were cut down by chainsaws

To make way for straighter and wider commercial arteries,

And the mighty root systems were burned or left to rot,

Though sometimes experts were called in to study

their chemical composition,

Or to measure the size of the holes they left in the ground,

In any case to gather information about them

That could take the place of the roots themselves

And prove more useful for society in general than the actual trees,

Which only benefited the locals.

The new arteries brought in opportunities and a kind of prosperity

That was welcome and invigorating and alleviated some misery;

But the pollution accompanying these gains,

And the expropriation of land in the path of the roads,

And the displacement of a large portion of the population,

And the commercialization of everything,

And the mechanization of everything,

Led to an inner desolation that affected the whole culture,

So that people moved about in the fog fearfully

With no clear sense of direction or purpose,

Each building a wall about his own plot of ground

and asserting his rights,

Or else banding together with others of like mind

to defend common interests

Over against the common interests of others,

equally likeminded.

All such groups perceived each other as enemies.

VIII

People could not hear each other very well in the fog.

Most finally gave up even trying to listen to those they were talking to

And simply yelled as loud as they could all at the same time,

Producing a muffled cacophony, like millions of rocks

thudding into sandbags.

Dialogue,

And what had once been known as the rational discussion of issues,

Fell into disuse,

A fact consistent with the irrational first principle of the society

But baffling for those who thought materialistic rationalism

Must lead to the reign of reason.

Law, conceived as the means to order, justice, and mutual responsibility,

Came to be construed legalistically as its moral basis evaporated,

Until finally laws and morality were taken to be synonymous

And court rulings were viewed by many citizens,

Often including legislators and judges,

As so many weapons for the obtainment of claims

Made by individuals or interest groups

Who knew how to use the damp climate to their own advantage.

Confusion, babble, and invective were everywhere,

And a great deal of killing went on under cover of the fog.

IX

In such a fog, how shall we love?

How shall we press another to our chest

As if all the world depended on her being there?

How is it possible to know a woman?

How is it possible to know a man?

Oh, tell us how our hands may touch another human being's cheeks

And wipe away her tears!

For if we are not loving, we are dead.

How frail we are!

Leaves that sift the wind,

Tap dance with the rain,

Glitter in the sun,

Until we grow old

And cannot grip any more,

And then, at a particular moment at the end of time,

As a gust shakes us

Or the cold enters our veins

Or the weight of night bears down on our worn-out frames,

We let go the branch and the tree

And the whole system of the tree

And drift down alone into darkness.

It is not possible to be fully alive,

It is not possible to give oneself fully to love,

If one believes that death is the end.

So great is the horror and sorrow at such a thought,

That those who harbor and nourish such a thought

Close down somewhere inside and harden their hearts

And say "no" to the fullness of life,

To commitment of the self to another and to others,

To love,

Out of fear of losing everything

And of suffering beyond endurance

When the object of the commitment dies,

Having no expectation of ever seeing the person again

Or of seeing justice done

Or of seeing misery brought to an end and redeemed.

Hope is the only soil in which true love can grow.

X

As the fog engulfed the oceans and continents,

People could not see each other's faces any longer.

They were too engrossed watching their own campfires,

And the glow of the flames was too feeble

For anyone to be able to make out clearly,

Or even to want to make out clearly,

The features of other human beings.

Only times of crisis brought a measure of clarity,

When storms ripped open the fog for a few moments,

Enabling the sophisticated barbarians

To catch sight of each other as persons

Before being gathered up again in gloom.

In the light of campfires that dotted the continents like glow-worms

One could make out only silhouettes and shadows,

Smudges on the haze,

Emaciated or obese,

Each detached from the rest.

No animals were anywhere to be seen,

Only their ingredients and products.

XI

A time came when the shrill babble arising from the fog ceased,

As if the machine that the world had become

Had been switched into neutral by an unknown hand.

A pause followed.

Then wheels of thunder rumbled above the fog,

As if artillery were being set in place.

Gigantic machinery clattered.

Then lightning exploded in the night,

Slashing the fog violently,

Stabbing the continents,

And fireballs the size of asteroids ignited everywhere

And roared over the earth,

Making mountains melt and oceans boil.

Then came rain,

Pinging on metal that was left,

Drumming on plastic that was left,

Pattering on black rocks,

Smacking on water.

For ages it rained and rained

Till all the flames were extinguished

And the steam dissipated

And the fog cleared away.

The world breathed quietly under the sun.

Then the people still living saw a rainbow in the sky

And a Figure on the horizon coming toward them

A radiant Figure coming closer

Coming . . .

Part V

Surely it is No Time for Poetry

Surely it is no time for poetry.

How dream when murder stalks

here there everywhere

murder

and the wind in the pines coming off the sea

carries only moans of the dying,

wails of the mourning?

How be enraptured by oleander flaring on roadsides

when each bloom is a rocket exploding

and the leaves are long knives cutting throats?

How grieve over personal loss

old age

the evaporation of the past

when everywhere and daily and always

are bombs/craters/body parts

eruption and corruption

whole populations scattered by greed

raped/ravaged/ruined

fleeing the destruction of everything theirs

the debris of what was ordinary life

now just smashed brick and charred wood?

All that is local, rooted, wild, old,

is going down before hubris

and being buried with millions of bodies

no one has use for.
Humans are mutating into flies
buzzing everywhere and nowhere
landing/leaving
here/there/nowhere
soiling windowpanes that look out on sky
leaving black specks on tablecloths
depositing maggots in carrion
and the rubbish heaps of cities
where rats and vermin live
and human beings no one has use for.

We have asphalted space
and sterilized time.
Today is great with nothing,
feeding on illusion.
The air is poisoned
and we have no time to breathe anyway.
Only blasted trees and preposterous towers
scratch the horizon of the future.

Surely it is no time for poetry.

I no longer hear the sound of the cricket,
the frog no longer croaks by the pond at night,
the crow has stopped cawing.
The white wolf will not lead its pack again

across the frozen snowfields of the north.
Ice floes shrink,
permafrost softens,
the home of the polar bear is melting.
Sea birds trapped in oil spills suffocate,
the ocean floor is poisoned.
In lakes foul weeds riot,
fish go belly-up.
Wild forests fall to the saw,
yellow metal monsters gut mountainsides,
orange flames turn prairies black.
Deserts eat up green land,
plagues bloom like algae in rivers,
insects hopping/crawling/flying
are on the march.

In a zoo in a city somewhere
a Bengalese tiger without offspring
paces up and down in its cage.

Nature is unnatured

Black is perpetrated and called white
or just is perpetrated and called nothing

Greed rules
murdermurder

Women strive to keep order and scavenge and are raped
murder
Children are born old or ill
they are orphaned/abducted/seduced
they shoot real guns
sold by snakes and spiders
murdermurder

Untimely warmth deceives buds.
Politicians cry "Spring, spring," when there is no spring—
frost then massacres the blossoms.

The adder lies coiled at the door,
the black widow has crawled into the house,
the scorpion lurks between the sheets of the bed.

Surely it is no time for poetry.

To the contrary—
surely it *is* a time for poetry.
When night falls, and the far-off beat
of drums draws near, we shall sing God's life
and ours, defeating darkness with our words.
Like rainclouds arising in a blue sky,
full of water for the desiccated earth,
our words arise in the heart of the Word
who makes all things out of silence.

It is time to speak, to cry out, to create.

We shall send our words in legions

against the raiders of villages

and the bombers of cities

who destroy the habitations of men

and slay women and children.

We shall praise the Creator,

who makes and remakes being

and all beings existing.

We shall lift him up in the teeth

of the snarling wolf and the hissing viper,

and they shall wither at his sight.

Words spoken out of light

are greater than drums beating

at night in the jungle:

life-bearers,

they carry God's power,

they carry *hope*—

and by *hope* in our Creator who is faithful,

we shall stand.

Surely it is a time for poetry

My Poems

As the world erupts, I sit in my garden
Writing poems. What have they to do
With the thousands slaughtered?

They are crystals of life set against negation,
Sparks popping out from the burning bush.

I sing of veined leaves,
Of stardust,
Of ants,
Of cows munching grass,
Of mice,
And of cats.

Cats kill mice, I know that;
But they do not slaughter.
Adam slaughters.
"Why not?" the self says perversely to temptation,
Defying order,
Defying reason.
Then, cut off from its oxygen tube,
It builds apparatuses to keep on breathing;
And when it starts to suffocate for want of air,
It stamps and swears,
Rages and blasphemes,

And slaughters.

I sing of geese in a wedge high over earth,
Pinions beating with metronomic precision,
Necks like cannon barrels aimed at the Arctic,
Feet stretched out taut,
Eyes undeviating, black,
Fixed fiercely on the single objective
Of hatching their young as their nature demands.

My poems say: "God is good,
His order is good."
I say to him and to his order: "Yes."
God *is.*
He is fire, he burns—
He burns but is not consumed.
And he *acts,*
He speaks being.
And he *saves,*
He saves from negation,
From the shadow that has no proper being,
Evil.
For evil is no thing,
It was not created;
It is unreason,
The good misshapen,
So it cannot be eternal.

It is *dis*order.
The Son of God stamped it down,
He confirmed its doom.

I sing of wild horses thundering on prairies,
Neighing and snorting,
Hooves pounding,
Nostrils flared,
Eyes wide, fierce,
Manes flying,
Tails like pennants going into battle.

Evil's progeny, death, is doomed—
Christ has risen!

I sing of whales plowing vast waters,
Pods in formation surfacing in the ocean,
Leviathans heaving up,
Heaving into air
Spouting,
Huge tails thrashing,
Their great backs gleaming like glaciated rock—
And they roll, plunge, and are gone.

My poems are buds on God's tree of life.
In the realm of the Spirit
They speak hope to those being slaughtered;

To the slaughterers they cry out:
"The evil you perpetrate is nothing;
The death you deal out has been defeated;
The perverse self you serve is doomed.
Die to it, look up,
Or you too will be nothing.
Embrace life."

The Cello (Song of Armenia)

The strokes on the cello draw a line through my heart,
A line like a plain full of rocks,
A line between earth and sky,
A horizon;
And across it tramp men
(Creatures in Christ's image),
Forms silhouetted on a cloud of blood,
Bent and curled like Armenian letters.

Back and forth across the taut strings
Moves the bow of the cello.
Letters spill out of the sound box
And flee across the plain to join their fellows,
Pursued by leaping hounds out of hell.
Many fall, some are torn to pieces,
But somehow they spring up again
And continue to run.
They wear black, carry shovels, hoes, books,
Musical instruments.
Most, half-dead, reach the edge of the earth
And join the host of letters.
As for the hounds out of hell,
The hunters,
They will be hunted in turn
When their day is done:

They will know the second death.
The letters will only die once;
Then they will turn into notes
And sing melodies to God.

Now violins give voice
And stream above the cello's bass.
The plain is full of rocks,
Memories of kingdoms.
Roundabout a crown of mountains,
Snowfields for diamonds:
They scintillate like shards of joy.
Cattle the color of the rocks,
Brown and black,
Graze among the monuments of stone.

"This is our land,
This is where our fathers lived
And herded cattle with sticks.
They lived in the shadow of the mountains
At the foot of snowfields
And collected water draining off the slopes.
They plowed and sowed,
Bent double like Armenian letters.
They hoed, reaped, feasted.
Here they married and bore children and died.
This is our land,

This is where our fathers suffered,
Worshipped,
Sang.
They walked on the tombs of their holy forbears
Buried in the floors of their stone churches,
Where candles flickering in the iron boxes of sand
Make yellow pools of wax
As they did long ago when our fathers' fathers quarried the rock
And built the churches with their domes like crowns
And carved their khachkar crosses on slabs of stone
And cut their sacred letters in the walls.
This is our land."

But now the violins stop playing,
The strain from the cello darkens.
The long line of silhouetted letters
Hunches against the sky.
Strange shapes lurch across the land.
I hear screeching,
Rasping,
The clamor of engines,
Cacophony.
Pipes strangle the plain,
Labyrinths of rusty worms.
Concrete slabs replace the khachkars,
I-beams the crosses.
Factories like rectangular mountains

Line the riverbanks.

Wires, cables, power lines

Tie up the air in knots.

Smokestacks nail the sky.

Cranes stalk among the derelict blocks,

Dinosaurs of iron,

Feeding with hooked teeth on oil drums, gas tanks, vats, troughs,

Concrete cisterns, metal bars, gears, wheel hubs, tires,

Carcasses of engines, trucks, tractors:

The ghosts of ancient empires, transmogrified.

Now even the cello has stopped playing.

For half an hour there is silence in heaven.

Then suddenly the cello starts up again

And the violins soar as though caught by a wind.

And look—the industrial bones begin to shake!

The pipes across the plain set to jigging,

The buildings start to quake,

The derricks roll and rattle.

The metal plates start banging,

The concrete slabs thump,

The oil drums heave,

The old machines cavort, belch, wheeze,

The smokestacks rock and toot.

Then lightning flashes like a signal

And the letters at the edge of the sky begin to dance.

The men in the long line drop their shovels,

They drop their hoes and books,

The musicians grab their fiddles and set to playing.

And now the sonorous line of the cello swells

And the violins unfurl their sails.

Across the plain great voices lift,

Song fills the earth.

The deep chords boom,

They echo like thunder on the mountains;

The high notes scale the air like hawks.

And far off on the distant horizon,

Where earth meets heaven,

The letters of the Armenian alphabet

Are busy carving words

In the cloud of clotted blood massed behind them:

> *"Hear you, all inhabitants of the earth:*
>
> *We have been raised up!*
>
> *We live!*
>
> *We dance!*
>
> *We sing!*
>
> *We praise our Creator God,*
>
> *We praise our Redeemer God.*
>
> *He is our God,*
>
> *We are his people.*

His name is carved on our brows
And in our hearts.
His love is forever.
Let him with ears to hear, hear."

Now the stillness of evening

Settles on the ancient plain,

As the shadows of the rocks grow long

And the orange light leaves the mountains.

The music of the cello fades:

"This is our land," it sings one last time.

"Here our fathers lived,

Raised their monuments of stone,

Praised their God.

Here they loved,

Suffered,

Died.

We belong here with them.

This is our land forever."

Oh Rwanda!

Oh, hills, hills, hills!
You country of a thousand hills,
You lie like a green sow on its side,
Your udders heavy,
Your swollen teats suckled by the hungry clouds!
Your back bristles with a million trees:
Looping up in the air, your palms are fireworks;
Your banana leaves, the teeth of combs
Smoothing breezes;
Your elegant eucalyptus are xylophones
Where winds play scales;
Your mimosas are the lashes of virgins,
The lips of lovers,
Quivering.

But, oh Rwanda—
I cannot forget your suffering!

Your patchwork plots across the hills
Are clad in color like your lovely women
With their black ivory arms
And skin like fresh black snow,
Striding down red country roads,
Heads piled high with produce,
Swaying majestically like candle flames—

But, oh people of Rwanda,
I cannot forget the killing!

Your men are pensive,
Their minds are haunted.
So many fewer than there used to be,
Wondering if they can cope,
Feed their families,
Find strength to build their homes,
To plant their crops,
Tend their herds,
Sell their products,
Build schools,
Train doctors,
Judge criminals,
Make laws,
Govern the nation.
Your men are sober, some wondering
If they can ever forgive;
Others—can they ever be forgiven?
Some no longer think about such things
And quickly smile
With large white teeth;
They laugh and joke;
But behind their eyes fear crawls like ants.

The killing—

Oh, you children of Rwanda!

"Where is Daddy?"

And where are so many of the mothers?

But life is like a green surge,

A root breaking rock!

The children sing and shout, they beat on drums,

They squirm and wriggle,

They squeal and run and fall,

Howl, bawl,

Run, fall, get up—oh, *yes!*

And roll their full-moon eyes

In their night-black faces,

And their mouths open up in smiles

Like coconut slices,

And they giggle like tumbling streams—

Oh, children of Rwanda, *may you live!*

May you grow into the fullness of your years!

Oh, breast the dawn, you young!

Greet great day!

Lift up your land!

Sing on the hills,

Sing with the birds!

Oh Rwanda!

Let all the colors of your trees and flowers and your gorgeous
women

Shout!

And may God's Spirit

Fall on you like harvest rain

And comfort you with all goodness and gladness

And water your harrowed hearts with hope

Forever and ever!

The Mountain

I

In a flat age, how tell of mountains?
How talk to residents of marshes
Of cloud-swaddling peaks
That penetrate azure
And reflect heaven?

"Reality is horizontal,"
They will say.
"Don't speak to us of heights and depths.
Verticality is a lie.
Unseen realms don't exist.
Truth is culturally relative.
Any other claim is mythical rubbish
Invented by people who live under bell-jars
And imagine things.
Such people should be shot.
There's no one over us or under us,
We're not responsible to anyone.
In this life get wealth and power,
If you can;
Get pleasure,
If you can.
Then die and rot."

So say the residents of marshes,

Who certainly don't live under bell-jars,

Do they?

How speak to such people of mountains?

II

Let us talk of snakes and *tsetse* flies,

Of crocodiles and crabs,

Of mud and fetid water

Where mosquitoes breed by billions.

Let us speak of parasites and worms,

Of muck and hacked-up corpses

A-crawl with maggots,

Of monstrous murders done in jungles

(And not only in jungles)

With machetes and machine guns

(Do you hear the stifled cries?)

On nights when the barbarous moon herself

Is off drinking blood under cover of dark

And cannot bear witness

(Can you imagine such a thing?).

III

We are ghosts walking beside ourselves,

Crunching numbers.

On the X-ray charts

You can see our wizened hearts

Held hostage by digits.

We are leeches clamped to virtual reality,

Believing we are sucking blood.

Technological fundamentalists,

We set up graven images made of dots

And bow before them.

Empty souled, we deny the existence of soul

To protect ourselves.

We camp in digital graveyards

And call it civilized living.

Self-deceived,

We call the abstract data we eat

"Food."

Grazing each other's surfaces,

We mistake information for knowledge,

Technical know-how for wisdom,

The accumulation of messages

For personal encounter.

Self-proclaimed conquerors of time and space,

We are the conquered ones,

Enslaved by the spatial and temporal compression

We have wrought.

As residents of marshes,

We sweat profusely

And spend a great deal of time each day
Applying insect lotion and scratching.
We walk beside ourselves,
Identified with our own one-dimensional shadows.
We live and die under bell-jars—
Stationary though appearing to move—
And this way of life we name "freedom."

The country roundabout here is flat.
Mounds are rare,
Hillocks scarce.
No mountains are anywhere to be seen.

IV

We do not believe in mountains.

V

I have seen a mountain.

VI

Let us talk of mountains.

VII

You walk for months, for years,
Till you begin to tire.

You leave behind the marshes,

The jungles.

You cross endless plains

endless

empty

plains.

You walk and walk,

Clouds above move ceaselessly,

You are like a cloud,

You move,

You cross endless plains,

You walk and walk.

You see far and wide,

But there is nothing to see far and wide.

You walk.

You move.

You walk and walk.

You begin to tire.

VIII

And then on the horizon you see clouds that don't move.

Their shapes are sharp like saw-teeth,

Which is odd for clouds.

You walk and walk,

The clouds still don't move—

That is odd.

Then you notice you are rising.

You look behind,

The plain is sinking.

You have new eyes.

The clouds ahead turn out to be stone.

Odd shapes:

Triangles and cones, humps, points, walls,

All in the vertical mode.

What is the vertical mode?

From now on,

To walk is to climb.

You have never climbed before.

You go *up*—

Up, not forward.

It is hard to go up.

The slope gets steeper and steeper.

You're climbing over rocks and loose gravel.

You're sliding,

You lurch,

You reach out

Clutch

Grab

You're scrambling

Rocks, scree

Falling

Rocks

Scree

Falling—

And suddenly cloud comes upon you
And envelops you—
And it is like the Spirit of God you don't believe in
Coming upon you—
And you are in a dark swirling tumult
And all is black and you see nothing
And behind you stones loosed by your climbing feet
Bounce and ricochet into the abyss
Careening, cracking
Their sound echoing off the vertical walls
Like the cries of lost souls
Plunging into hell

"Help me!"

Wind sweeps your words up
Into that other dimension
That didn't exist—
And you look
Up
And struggle
Up
And are lifted
Up

And the clouds above shred and are rent
Like the curtain in the temple of Jerusalem
When the Lord Jesus died.
You break through the shrouds of night
And emerge into blue peace,
Blue of oceans you have never known,
Of distances you have never thought:
Blue of Alpha and Omega:
Blue of *God*.

Here on the mountain
Is original silence
Into which God speaks his word
And the Word is in the silence
And the Word is the silence
And the Word and the silence are one

www.ingramcontent.com/pod-product-compliance
Lightning Source LLC
Chambersburg PA
CBHW060403090426
42734CB00011B/2249